Looking Back

NIAGARA-ON-THE-LAKE

ONTARIO

Dedicated to
Ethna, Evan, Gwenyth, Eric, Stuart & David

Niagara has always had a strong connection to the British Monarchy, as this photograph can attest. In 1901 hundreds of people lined King Street to catch a glimpse of the Duke and Duchess of Cornwall (future King George V and Queen Mary) leaving Niagara. The couple is seen here on the wooden platform with a carpet on it; they are about to leave Niagara by train.

Looking Back

NIAGARA-ON-THE-LAKE

ONTARIO

Clark Bernat and Joy Ormsby

Looking Back Press

Vanwell Publishing acknowledges the financial support of the Government of Canada through the Book Publishing Industry Development Program for our publishing activities.

Published by Looking Back Press
An Imprint of Vanwell Publishing Limited
1 Northrup Crescent, P.O. Box 2131
St. Catharines, ON L2R 7S2
For all general information contact Looking Back Press at:
Telephone 905-937-3100 ext. 835
Fax 905-937-1760
E-Mail vanessa.mclean@vanwell.com

For customer service and orders:
Toll-free 1-800-661-6136

Printed in Canada
11 10 09 08 07   5 4 3 2

National Library of Canada Cataloguing in Publication

Bernat, Clark, 1974-
    Niagara-on-the-Lake, Ontario / Clark Bernat and Joy Ormsby.

(Looking back)
ISBN 1-55068-928-2

    1. Niagara-on-the-Lake (Ont.)—History—Pictorial works.
I. Ormsby, Joy, 1928- II. Title. III. Series: Looking back (St. Catharines, Ont.)

FC3099.N54B47 2003   971.3'38   C2003-906315-1

Between 1937 and 1940, the Niagara Parks Commission and the federal government undertook the restoration of Fort George as a make-work project. The official re-opening, organised by Lou Cahill, occurred in June 1950. The photograph shows part of the crowd of 10,000 who attended the ceremony.

Contents

Acknowledgements

We are indebted to the Niagara Historical Society, whose archives provided most of the photographs in this book and to those people who donated the originals to the Museum. We also thank Margo Fyfe, Isabelle Ridgeway, Ronald Dale, Al Davey, Donald Combe, Fred Habermehl, and others for proofreading sections of the manuscript and offering advice, and Jim Smith, Sylvia Lavelle, Joan Elliott and everybody else we asked to help identify subjects in the group photographs. Isabelle's *Sailing out of Niagara*, the Joseph Masters collection at the Niagara-on-the-Lake Public Library, and of course, Janet Carnochan's *History of Niagara* were tremendously helpful for information. Thanks also to the Niagara Historical Society's premier summer student, Amy Klassen for help with the data processing.

Introduction

Generations of Native Canadians lived in the Niagara region for centuries before the first permanent settlers arrived during the American Revolution. These native people gave the river the name Niagara.

In the winter of 1778-1779, Butler's Rangers, a Loyalist Regiment, came from the overcrowded Fort Niagara to build barracks here and the following year a few of their families began farming. The community multiplied after the Revolutionary War ended, when hundreds of disbanded Rangers and other Loyalist refugees occupied land granted as a reward for their loyalty to King George III. In 1791 an area near the mouth of the Niagara River, now the town of Niagara-on-the-Lake, was surveyed for a town site.

In 1792 the pioneer village of Niagara became the first capital of Upper Canada and the site of the first five sessions of the legislature. With this elevated political status came a military presence, a prosperous mercantile component, and elements of sophistication, including some fine houses and the province's first library, newspaper, and Freemason lodge.

The town survived the removal of the capital to "Muddy York,", retaining its strong military and merchant elements, but was devastated in the 1812-1814 war. A battle site in 1813 and occupied by enemy troops for seven months, Niagara was deliberately torched when the Americans and their Canadian Volunteer supporters retreated in December 1813.

The rebuilding, begun at the end of the war, started an economic boom which, reinvigorated in the 1830s and 1840s by the activities of the Niagara Harbour and Dock Company, lasted for 35 years. The town's population grew to over 3,300, merchants benefitted from a busy trans-shipping trade, and the second courthouse, built in 1817, drew lawyers and civil servants to the town.

However, the second Welland Canal, which opened in the mid-1840s, bypassed Niagara, effectively killing the trans-shipping business and the Dock Company, the town's largest employer. The town slipped into a recession and by 1871 the population had plummeted to 1,600.

In the 1870s, the tide turned—at least in the summer months—when visitors to the elegant Queen's Royal Hotel (opened in 1869) and citizen-soldiers training at Camp Niagara swelled the local population. This new period of prosperity continued until the end of the First World War when another recession began, lasting until the late 1950s.

In the 1960s economic recovery based on heritage, the Shaw Festival and local wineries began. This recovery continues.

With the exception of a few early portraits, the photographs in this book were taken between the 1850s and the 1950s. We arranged them into six chapters to illustrate important aspects of life in Niagara.

Chapter One features photographs of the Queen Street commercial district from 1870 to 1949 as well as several nineteenth century and early twentieth century hotels. Portraits of merchants and innkeepers are also included. Several of the shops shown represent the 1817-50 growth period, others the late nineteenth-century boom. Some of the latter replaced buildings destroyed by a fire on the north side of the street in 1886. Taverns and hotels have done well in Niagara— except for a brief period in the 1920s and 1930s when several went bankrupt.

Chapter Two looks at the churches, schools and other voluntary organisations and their members, who made important contributions to community life. Group photographs are included.

Chapter Three illustrates the means of transportation—particularly lake boats and steam trains—and their facilities at the harbour and dock area. Boats and trains were vital to the town's prosperity prior to the advent of affordable automobiles.

Chapter Four focuses on houses built before 1840, whose restoration preserved the town's heritage, as well as the grand houses built or refurbished in the late nineteenth century. Niagara retains the best stock of pre-1840 houses in the province. The choice of houses included in Chapter Four was determined by availability of pre-1955 photographs.

Chapter Five features sports and recreational activities offered for both residents and tourists. Local athletes and the international tournaments held in Niagara are also mentioned. Whether it was winter or summer, hockey or golf, lawn bowling or tennis, Niagara had a little something for everyone.

Chapter Six is devoted to the importance of the military in the town. Niagara's military tradition predates early photography. We have tried to record some early military buildings by including later photographs showing them in a derelict state. Also included in this chapter are several photographs from the 1860s Fenian Raid period and many from Camp Niagara, a "summer feature" on the commons from the 1870s until the Second World War.

One
Queen Street
Enterprises and Hotels

MEMORIAL CLOCK TOWER, NIAGARA-ON-THE-LAKE, ONTARIO, CANADA.

Probably the most prominent structure on Queen Street is the cenotaph and clock tower. After much controversy about its form and location—settled by a plebiscite—the cenotaph was unveiled in 1922 as a memorial to ten local residents who gave their lives in the First World War. The architect, Charles Wilmot of Toronto, based his design on the campanile of St. Mark's Venice. Total cost of the 42 foot tower, including architectural fees, imported clock and fire alarm, was $8,165. A 1947 rededication ceremony commemorated residents killed in the Second World War, whose names were added to the original ten.

QUEEN ST.

This 1870 view of the south side of Queen Street shows, from right to left: John Lees Alma's upscale grocery and wine store, originally built in 1825 for dry goods merchant John Daly; an early narrow frame building, the business of John McMillan and his son Dave; the hotel of James Walsh and his son Frank, which was built *c.*1840 as half shop, half house; the Sherlock block, built *c.*1850 as two buildings and later joined with a "boomtown" front added to disguise the joining; the Court House, and the oldest building in the commercial area, William Duff Miller's 1817 stationery shop. The second storey was added in 1855, probably by grocer Henry Chrysler. Purchased by the LCBO in 1928, the building was restored in 1973.

The same streetscape over 100 years later seems, at first glance, remarkably similar. However, there are significant changes. The Alma store was reconstructed in 1981, a project that won an Ontario Renews award for its owners. The adjoining three-story red-brick building on the site of the former McMillans' shop was part of the reconstruction. On the other hand, despite their newer shop fronts, the Walsh hotel and the Sherlock block retain much of their original character. These buildings, along with the Court House, and William Duff Miller's store are designated buildings of major importance to a streetscape that was described by London architect Nicholas Hill, in 1986, as part of "one of the finest historic streets in the nation." (Photograph courtesy of Jim Alexander)

The most impressive building in the downtown business area, the 1847 Court House, was
built as part of the town's effort to remain the county seat. The Classical Revival building was designed by architect William Thomas, who also designed St. Michael's Cathedral,
St. Lawrence Hall, and the Don Jail in Toronto, as well as Grace United Church in
Niagara-on-the-Lake. The building included elaborate court rooms, prisoner cells, a
market hall and a speakers' balcony above the front entrance. Two local contractors, master
carpenter John Davidson and mason John Thornton were in charge of the construction.

QUEEN ST.

In 1862, after St. Catharines became the county seat, Niagara's Court House was adapted
to local functions. Its main use was the Town Hall, but on occasion it also served as market,
bank, post office, fire hall, library, suspender factory and a little theatre. This 1905
photograph shows local firemen at the front entrance.

This photograph shows Queen Street in 1905. The generous 99-foot width of the unpaved, tree-lined main street was established by the 1794 plan of the town. The trees were courtesy of Mayor Henry Paffard, who, *c.*1865, persuaded the town council to grant $25 to start a tree-planting scheme. The automobiles were predictors of things to come, but three livery stables survived in town until the 1920s.

Mayor W.H. Harrison posed with the paving crew on King Street in the summer of 1914. In the fall, Queen Street was paved. (Photograph courtesy of Mr. Donald Harrison)

This view shows the south side of Queen Street *c*.1939. James Connolly's china store and ice cream parlour stands at the corner of King Street. The clapboard building was George A. Clement's residence in the 1830s. Next door, part of the roof of the 1911 Fire Hall is visible. Set back from the street, it was later converted to stores. The Clement store, established in 1850, was located next to the Fire Hall. Note its flat-roofed addition, which was added in the 1890s. By 1905 the Clement store was Librock's stationery, jewellery, and china store. Adjacent to the Clement Store, the narrow three-story The Sign of the Pineapple was built *c*.1830 and mostly used as a grocery by Steven Follett, Fred Best, and Dick Allen. Hedley and Doug Reid owned the store during the Second World War. Note the soldiers on the sidewalk and the 1937-38 Pontiac parked at the front. A Gothic Revival storefront was added in the 1970s when the store became an upscale specialty shop.

John Lees Alma (1799-1890), Queen Street merchant, came to Niagara around 1830 after travelling the world for years, living aboard ships. A daughter, Emily Joanna was born in Valparaiso, Chile in 1828. His first wife, Emily died in Niagara in 1841 at the age of 38. Of his eight children only one survived him. In 1871 he and his second wife Elizabeth Hissock (m. 1849), who was herself an orphan, took in one of Maria Rye's girls, Mary Ann Cook (age 13), raising her as one of the family. Alma's Store originally had the "T" sign above the door signifying that he sold provisions (food, tea, coffee, wines, etc.).

Steven H. Follett (1818-1887), proprietor of the Queen Street store, now known as the Sign of the Pineapple, then known simply as Folletts, served twenty-two years on Council, including one term as Mayor (1881). A supporter of the temperance movement in the 1850s, he signed a petition to prohibit the manufacture and sale of alcoholic beverages because they were responsible for "pecuniary sacrifice, mental and physical maladies, outrages on life and property, and moral contamination."

15

This 1939 photograph shows the drugstore of E.W. Field at the corner of King Street. Next to it stood the town's first telephone exchange— a two-story, pink brick, flat-roofed 1890s building where customers could make calls to Toronto and Buffalo. It was converted to a dwelling after 1950 and to a store in the 1970s. The solid two-story brick building next door was built *c.*1895 by local builder Walter Campbell for barber Louis Frank, a former sergeant of the 12th U.S. Infantry, noted for his fine pair of side-whiskers. Fred Curtis succeeded Mr. Frank. Next to the barber shop, a building was created from the two separate front gabled units—possibly a house and a store—joined in 1860. From 1914 to the 1950s, one part of the building was a fruit and grocery store owned in succession by Frank Riley, A. R. DaConza, and Peter Marino. The second part was a restaurant that was owned by Charlie Sherlock in the First World War, followed by Vern Davey, Mary Spencer, and Lee Shuk. A large, two-story, red brick building known as the Rowley block anchors the northern part of Queen Street. This building was a late Victorian adaptation of the Italianate style built in 1894 by Walter Davidson for S.B. Rowley, an American businessman.

The Rowley block has accommodated a variety of tenants, including the Post Office. Postmaster Joe Healey, his assistant, and his dog pose at the entrance around1920.

In the late 1860s Henry Paffard moved his apothecary business into the newly-renovated building at the corner of King Street. He was the first of a series of druggist-owners including John De W. Randall, A.J. Coyne, and E.W. Field. Field retired in 1964. The building, restored mainly through the efforts of the Niagara Foundation, reopened in 1971 as a museum dedicated to the history of pharmacology. It is operated and maintained by the Ontario College of Pharmacy.

5 QUEEN ST.

Henry Paffard (1834-1912), pharmacist, was the town's longest serving mayor (twenty-three years). He was also a keen horticulturist and we are indebted to him for the shade trees on our streets and in Simcoe Park. In his garden at the corner of Victoria Street, next to Grace United Church (now the site of the Shaw Wine Bar), he grew grapes, peaches, and figs. A plaque on the façade of the Court House pays tribute to his civic contributions.

John De W. Randall came to Niagara as an assistant to Henry Paffard at the apothecary, succeeding Paffard as owner in 1895. He served three years as Mayor, was District Deputy Grand Master of the Masonic Lodge, Warden of St. Mark's Church, and the meteorological observer for Niagara. At his funeral in March 1914, flags flew at half-mast on both public and private buildings, businesses closed, and citizens lined the route of the cortege.

Lewis Clement (1787-1879), a veteran of the battles of Queenston Heights and Chippawa in the War of 1812, was one of the town's early merchants in 1825. In 1831 he became a director of the Niagara Harbour and Dock Company and built "the new commodious" store at Queen and Victoria streets. Bankrupted by the failure of the Dock Company, he apparently worked as a labourer to pay his debts. He is said to have walked from Niagara to Fort Erie in 1866 at the age of 79.

Bert McClelland Jr., one of the younger generations of McClellands who owned the store built by Lewis Clement, served as a sergeant in the Fort Garry Horse with the Canadian Expeditionary Force in France in the First World War.

The brick store at the corner of Regent and Queen was built in 1845, partly on the foundation of an earlier store. Thomas M. Rowland had a dry goods and custom tailoring shop here for twenty years. He was followed by Robert Burns and then by Fred Rowland, who was owner at the time of this 1902 photograph. William Greaves bought the store (then vacant) in 1927 and began a very successful marmalade and jam-making business that actually expanded during the Depression. _55 QUEEN ST._

For over 30 years, prior to the First World War, this 1840s building known as the Old Bakery was the bake shop of Mel Slingerland, followed by Mr. Gardner, James McPhee and Ned Patterson and his sons Eddie and Bill, who baked their bread on bricks (c.1914). The McKenzies later opened a plumbing, electric, and heating business here, adding gasoline pumps on the premises in 1924.

The owner of this timber frame building of the 1860s was popular with the town's children, who called him "Candy" Evans. In the 1980s it became part of the Prince of Wales complex—a well-conserved historic structure amidst the new brick and clapboard Picton Street hotel extension. This photograph of Evans Ice Cream and Candy Store is c.1910. Shown from left to right are Mrs. Parker, Lillian Parker and Mrs. Matthews.

James Carnochan, carpenter, built this house at the corner of Wellington and Picton Streets in 1845. The family owned it until 1892 when Janet Carnochan sold it to John de Witt Randall. One of the last homes to remain in the main commercial area, it became the restaurant of the Royal Park Hotel in the late 1980s.

The above photograph of the commercial block on King Street in 1890 shows the water tower, Mike Greenes' livery stable (shown in close-up below), the Pacific Hotel, the rear of George A. Clement's Queen Street building, and across the road, the front of the apothecary. The Pacific, built *c.*1850 at the South East corner of Market Street, was replaced in 1914 by the station for the Niagara, St. Catharines, and Toronto Railway Company. A section of the old hotel was moved to form part of number 66 Prideaux Street.

This 1898 photograph was taken from one of the upper levels of the Court House on Queen Street and looks down onto the market area behind the Alma Block. In the left foreground is the Angel Inn, in the middle is Grace United Church. The spire of St. Andrew's Church can be seen to the left of the photograph on the horizon and in the middle of the horizon is the Chautauqua Hotel. This view shows the distance that visitors to the Chautauqua area are from town; as well, we have a rare glimpse of the backyards of some of the homes on the side streets and Queen Street. Note the laundry on the line attached to the outhouse behind one of the businesses.

In the 1830s the town flourished. It was the legal centre of Lincoln, Welland, and Haldimand counties and the location of the busy Niagara Harbour and Dock Company, its largest employer. It was also the location of about twenty-eight taverns, including Richard Moffat's inn (on the left in this *c.*1900 photograph) and James Miller's hotel (on the right), both <u>built in 1835.</u> By the end of the century Jimmy Doyle owned both hotels. The Moffat still operates as an inn. Jay Doyle tore down the Miller in the 1930s.

60 Picton St.

William Long built the brick hotel at the <u>corner of King and Picton streets in 1881.</u> In 1899 P.J. O'Neil bought Long's Hotel and renamed it The Niagara House. According to tradition, its present name, the Prince of Wales, was bestowed in honour of a royal visit to the town. In the early 1900s rooms rented for six dollars per night, which would be equivalent to approximately $125 today.

6 Picton St

The Whale Inn, shown in this 1910 photograph, was built in 1835 to cater to sailors and merchants arriving at the Melville St. harbour. The Whale Inn is also known as the Elliott House. Its first innkeeper, Walter Elliott, was succeeded by his son Thomas, a fisherman, whose wife and daughters ran a boarding house here post 1870. The Elliott House was noted for the excellence of its cooking; visitors to the nearby Queen's Royal Hotel often ate there. Though Elliotts was supposedly a teetotal establishment, its house mincemeat was liberally laced with brandy and sherry. For many years the house has been a private dwelling, but the taproom door at the left front is a reminder of its earlier function.

66 KING ST.

This view of the mouth of the Niagara River depicts the famous Whale Inn view, one of the best in Ontario. The painting is a c.1856 watercolour by Owen Staples from a pencil sketch by Francis Grainger.

This inn was built in 1860 by John Thornton for one of the principals of a railway car company at the dock and named Baker's Niagara House. In 1870 John Rousseau Sr. bought the establishment and renamed it Lakeview House. His son John Jr. inherited the business in 1881, and for the following twenty years leased it to a series of innkeepers, including Mrs. Long. During her tenancy, a spark from a passing C.S.R. train set fire to the roof. Contractor for the repair-renovation, which included the addition of a third story, was Walter Davidson. Later owners included Jay Doyle and Frank Addison. It was the only hotel in Niagara that remained open year-round in 1934. Over the years, the Lakeview was renamed the Riverside and then the Harbour Inn. It burned in the late 1990s.

In the 1860s Captain Duncan Milloy, master of a lake boat, enlarged a small house built in 1822 by Mary Trumble. His son Captain Bill Milloy opened the residence as The Oban Hotel in 1895 after making extensive renovations. The Oban was reconstructed in 1993 after a devastating fire on Christmas night 1992.

160 FRONT ST.

Captain Duncan Milloy was owner of the *City of Toronto*, the last steamboat launched at Niagara. After much controversy, Captain Milloy bought the property of the old Niagara Harbour and Dock Company for $7,000. This gave his family prime dock space at Niagara for decades. He died at his home, Oban House, in 1871 at the age of 46.

Opened in 1869, the Royal Niagara was built with money received from the County after the relocation of the Court House to St. Catharines. The first-class hotel became the destination of choice for those who wanted to escape the confines of the city and enjoy a peaceful time by the lake. The Royal Niagara was one of the finest hotels in North America. The hotel later changed its name to the Queen's Royal Hotel.

This is the view of the Queen's Royal Hotel from Front Street around 1895. This wonderful hotel became the victim of a rollercoaster economy based on tourism. Advancements in roads and cars led to the demise of the Queen's Royal in 1927. The building was demolished in 1930. The site is now a favourite picnic spot.

QUEEN'S ROYAL PARK

Above is a view of the Queen's Royal Hotel Rotunda, below the dining room. An advertisement from 1893 states, "The rooms of the Queen's Royal are high and well ventilated, the corridors, parlours and drawing-rooms are spacious [and] handsomely furnished. In the evening the whole is lit up by electricity. A flight of steps leads down to the private dock of the hotel, whereat the little pleasure steamers call, and in front of which is the anchorage of the Royal Canadian Yacht Club, the largest on fresh waters."

In 1901, anticipating a Royal visit, the Queen's Royal Hotel installed an acetylene gas plant in order to light the rooms. Unfortunately on October 12 when the future King George V and Queen Mary were at the Queen's the gas leaked, forcing the Royal party to sit on the verandah until 3 A.M. Seen here looking displeased are the future King and Queen and Lord and Lady Minto.

These people are posing underneath the wonderful horticultural arches made for the visit of the future King and Queen of England (Duke and Duchess of Cornwall) in 1901. Several of the arches decorated Front Street from the Queen's Royal Hotel to King Street. The Duke and Duchess must have been impressed by these beautiful sculptures as they rode in their carriage from the hotel to the train to depart Niagara.

The Niagara Assembly or Canadian Chautauqua was constructed in the mid-1880s. According to a newspaper report of 1887, "The object of the Assembly is to make this a place of popular resort—a people's institution, not an expensive one—which will contribute to the intellectual development of its visitors by carrying out the Chautauqua literary and scientific course of study." The Assembly also sold lots in the area for people interested in building cottages to stay for the summer. The Amphitheatre (below) was built to seat 3,000 people, with room for an additional 1,000 should it be necessary.

The Chautauqua Assembly was established as a resort for all ages. These youths are from Canada and the United States. No doubt Niagara offered a variety of experiences for these young men.

This is a view from one of the upper storeys of the Chautauqua Hotel, looking towards Niagara. The spire of St. Andrew's can be seen on the horizon. This shows how the Chautauqua Assembly was very much separated from the town at the time. The hotel burned down in 1909.

Two
Community

The congregation of St. Andrew's Church was established by 1794. *The Gleaner* of 1831 states that the first church was on the site of the present church. The original church was destroyed in 1813 when the American forces retreated from the town and set it ablaze. Construction of the present Church of St. Andrew's (above) began on May 31, 1831. James Cooper was the architect of the building, which mirrors the New England influence on many of the homes that were built in town after the War of 1812. This picture was taken just before 1878; note the buggy shed to the left of the church. *PRESBYTERIAN*

323 SIMCOE ST.

Members of St. Andrew's Church are treated to one of the most stunning pulpits in the area. The pulpit and sounding board were fashioned by John Davidson, a local cabinet maker, and were a gift from member and benefactor John Young. When the new church was complete, pews went to the highest bidder. The least expensive pew went for £8 and the most expensive went to Jared Stocking for £40.

Rev. MacFarlane (1870-1935) was minister of St. Andrew's Church 1930–35) During the Depression, the offering plate often held as little as $20 and at one point the Church could not even afford the phone bills. This scholarly, genial preacher saw the congregation through the rough times until his sudden death in 1935. He was the first to be buried in the "ministers' plot."

It has been traditionally understood that construction of the impressive stone walls of St. Mark's Church began in 1804 and were completed in 1809, but it may have been earlier. During the War of 1812, the church was used as an emergency British hospital and burned by the retreating American forces in December of 1813. The rebuilt church was consecrated in 1828, a year before the death of its first minister, Reverend Robert Addison. The transepts and tower of the church were added in 1839. ___ANGLICAN.___

___BYRON ST.___

Renovations to mark the centennial of St. Mark's Church in 1892 consisted of removing the galleries and modernizing the box pews. The high pulpits seen on each side of the chancel remain to this day.

The Methodist congregation in Niagara-on-the-Lake built its first church on Gate Street in 1823. The Canada Presbyterian Church on Victoria Street, shown here *c.*1900, was purchased by them in 1875 for $1,600. The building became <u>Grace United Church</u> in 1925 when the Congregational, Presbyterian, and Methodist Churches united.

220 VICTORIA ST

Local photographer W. Quinn took this photograph of the interior of the Methodist Church on Victoria Street on Easter Sunday, 1897. Each member of the choir received a copy. The interior and exterior of this church required major renovations in 1875. The work took two years and $750 to complete. The Methodists met in the Temperance Hall until renovations were finished.

Subscription lists started in 1831 for the construction of the first Catholic Church in Niagara. The first church service was held in 1834. Pews were not added to the Church until 1844 at an expense of £29. The photograph shows the building *c.*1900.

ST VINCENT de PAUL CHURCH   93 PICTON ST.

The church presbytery or "Glebe House" was built in 1834. Contributions were obtained from members of all congregations in town for the cost of construction. This building remained next to St. Vincent de Paul Church on Picton Street until 1890 when the current rectory was constructed. The presbytery was moved to Platoff Street where it was used as a private home until the 1960s. (Photograph courtesy of Miss Patricia McCarthy)

This four-room building at Platoff and Davy streets, built by master mason John Thornton in 1859, was the first permanent schoolhouse in the town. Earlier schools, many of them private, were housed in temporary quarters. This 1859 building was superseded by Parliament Oak School on King Street in 1949.

Pupils posing at the front door in this 1921 photograph, are, from left to right, (front row) Ed Doyle, Nixon Brennan, Harry Matthewson, and Norm Doherty; (middle row) Peter Riches, Grace Dalgleish, M. Hindle, T. Bradley, M. McClelland, E. Masters, and D. Appleford; (back row) Albert Ball, Bert Hall, Roy Campbell, Nelson Gordon, Red Campbell, Harry Sherlock, Fred Curtis, Gordon Campbell, and George Curtis.

Although the seal of the Niagara County Grammar School reads "Established 1808," this 1875 building at Davy and Castlereagh streets was its first permanent home. After the school closed in 1947 the building became an annex to the museum. The new high school did not open until 1956. In the interim, the town and township purchased secondary education from Stamford and Niagara Falls, deciding to build a new school only after cost per pupil rose to $460 per year.

Posing here are the six members of the 1947 graduating class of the old high school. Pictured from left to right are the following: (kneeling) Ferguson Phelps, (standing) Bernice Thompson, Ethel Gill, Mary Barnes, Janet Webster, and Aileen Cumpson.
This was the last class at the school.

Posing with Mr. Bale (the high school principal from 1914-22) in April 1921, are, from left to right, (front row) Genevieve Bale, Phyllis Brown, Margaret Morgan, Ida Walsh, Ruth Lee, and Ruth Casselman; (middle row) Zaida Lutz (m. Don Harrison), Dolly Bishop, Aida Casselman, Kate Carnochan (m. Caughill), Albert Davey, Leo Switzer, Winston Bishop, E.W. Field, George Martin, Albert Reid, and Wallace Brown; (back row) Gladys Field, Monica McGinn, Zella Lutz, Doris Redhead, Catherine Mathewson, Glen Bishop, Jimmy Doyle, Dick Speckman, Archie Cross, Ellison Brown, Don Harrison, Herb Switzer, and Mr. Bale.

In 1869, the second Court House building in Niagara was purchased by Miss Maria Rye and was called "Our Western Home." Miss Rye was upset with the living conditions of poor children on the streets of England and used the home to start a better life for them. The school operated from 1869 until just before the First World War and thousands of children, mostly girls, found new homes in Canada. This is one of the first groups of children who came to Miss Rye's Home in Niagara.

When it was completed in 1818, the second Court House was considered to be one of the finest buildings in Canada. It was used as a Court House and jail until 1847. Located on the outskirts of town, it was the site of many significant events including the Moseby Affair of 1837. Solomon Moseby was an escaped slave from Kentucky who was imprisoned while the government decided whether to send him back to Kentucky for the theft of his master's horse. A riot ensued; two men, Herbert Holmes and Jacob Green were killed, and Moseby disappeared for many years. This is how the building looked during Miss Rye's occupancy.

Heritage: When it was built in 1817 at the top of King Street, in what ow Rye Park, the town's second courthouse was deemed to be one of province's most impressive buildings. It fell into disuse after the third thouse was constructed on Queen Street in 1847. It wasn't until 1869 ouilding was occupied by Miss Maria Rye and was called Our Western e, a home that was organized to find homes in rural Ontario for girls some boys) from England who were in institutions for the needy in country. It closed in 1913 and the building was torn down shortly after-.

Photo provided by the Niagara Historical Society

emaining until the District School Board of Niagara decides Niagara District Secondary School's fate, council is working out ways to save the town's only high school.

Although time is no longer on their side, councillors decided to wait one more week to vote on a questionnaire for residents, asking what they are prepared to do to help keep NDSS open.

of time. We're not doing anything for NDSS and we need to be putting butts in those seats," said an obviously frustrated Mazza. "That's the only thing the DSBN cares about right now. This questionnaire won't change the numbers or the parameters set up. They have a mandate and we are not fighting the right fight by doing this."

The board has set October 30 as the date

school open.

The questionnaire p pared by the NDSS pl ning committee incl ing Councillor G Zalepa Jr. first ask: NDSS should rem open.

It then outlines f options regarding secondary school elementary school si tion the town is fac with a variety of sce ios that include kee NDSS open and relo ing Col. John Bu

The Masonic Lodge was one of the first buildings erected after the town was surveyed in 1791. A very important building in the infant community, it was the venue of church services, agricultural society meetings, and the opening of the first session of the first Parliament of Upper Canada. The original lodge was burned in 1813. The new building, erected on the site in 1816, was used as a store, a school, and a military barracks until the 1870s when the Freemasons bought the barracks and refitted it, thus returning to their original site. _153 KING ST. AT PRIDEAUX_

Many early settlers were Masons. Seen here is George A. Clement (d. 1884) in Masonic regalia. His son John A. Clement negotiated the resale of the Lodge property in the 1870s. The Clements were well known Queen Street merchants.

Memorial Hall (left) opened on June 4, 1907, to house the historical collection of the Niagara Historical Society. This is the first purpose-built museum building in Ontario. The Society had previously occupied a room on the third floor of the Court House on Queen Street. Local citizens and government helped raise $5,000 to build the Museum. The old high school (right) was built in 1875 and became part of the Museum complex shortly after the Second World War.

Visitors to the Niagara Historical Society Museum in the early years were treated to a wonderful collection of local photographs, documents, and artefacts from the long history of the town. Visitors were bombarded with Niagara's past. The early curator and longtime president of the Society, Janet Carnochan, worked extremely hard at establishing a very fine array of materials to interpret the early history of one of Ontario's oldest settlements. She ran the Society and its collection from 1895 until her death in 1926. This photograph was taken in July of 1927.

The signature artifact at the Niagara Historical Museum for over 100 years has been the cocked hat of Sir Isaac Brock. Brock never did wear the hat, which he ordered before the Battle of Queenston Heights. His nephew, who was stationed at Ball's Mills, brought it to Upper Canada after Brock's death at Queenston and presented it to George Ball of Locust Grove, Niagara before leaving the Mills. It was placed on the coffin of the late General during two of his interments at Queenston Heights where it was "fingered and tried on by so many people as to leave it in its present shabby state," according to one account.

Founded in 1800, the first circulating library in Ontario was the Niagara Library. The books were housed in many different buildings before settling into the Court House in 1895. The spacious room, once the Market Building, had Doric pillars that formerly marked the position of stalls. Mr. Paffard, Dr. Anderson, and Mr. R.C. Burns were instrumental in undertaking the move to a permanent home. This photograph shows the interior of the Library c.1930. The Library remained in the Court House until 2000.

Niagara Fire Co. No. 1 was chartered in 1830. By 1891 the company was divided into two divisions of seventeen men each. Pictured here are the men of B Co. in their new uniforms. Volunteer Firemen not only provided a vital service, they also organised the annual Labour Day events, which were very popular with the youth of the town.

In 1910 "future firemen" (including Albert and John Davey) pose with the old pumper outside the fire hall, then located in the Court House. A portion of the ladder wagon can be seen in the right rear corner. (Photograph courtesy of Mrs. Ruth Hawley)

This photograph of the interior of the Court House around 1904 shows the fire department's quarters. The sleeping room is through the door on the right. This photograph is from a tourist brochure, no doubt attempting to show that the fire department is well equipped to handle any emergencies.

This photograph shows the Niagara fire department and their equipment c.1900. The Court House is in the background. (Photograph courtesy of Mrs. Ruth Hawley)

In 1911 the fire department moved from the Court House to a new building to the east on Queen Street, shown here in 1921. (Photograph courtesy of Miss Patricia McCarthy)

In 1926 local firemen participated in a convention held on the commons. Posing here with their equipment are: T. Watt, J. Elliot, D. Sherlock, J. Stark, H. Schmidt, and J. Courtney. (Photograph courtesy of Niagara-on-the-Lake Fire Department)

The Niagara-on-the-Lake Fire Department Band is seen here posing on the steps of the Court House in 1912. (Photograph courtesy of Mr. E.A. Hunter)

A group photograph of the Niagara Fruit Growers Band, from left to right, as follows: (first row) W. H. Burtch, J.A. Stevens (second row) J. A. High, C.W. Jacob, A.C. Crysler, G.F. Willett, L.H. Collard, G.R. Mason, G.W. Sandham, F.M. Crysler Sr., and R. Slingerland (third row) W.J. Stirling, J.M. Crysler Jr., R.M. Crysler, A. Lahmer, C. Slingerland, C.W. Slingerland, and C.S. Knox (fourth row) F.W. Willett, R.H. Field, and H. Dunkelley.

The Niagara Boy Scouts visited the Buffalo Zoo in the 1940s. Standing, from left to right, are Fredrick Curtis, Alex Massey, unidentified, Allen Young, Bill Fowler, John Albrechtsen, Armond Haley, Glen Young, Leno Mori, Doug Young (Scoutmaster), Jim Currie, Reg Lavell, Percy Howse, and Eugene Lamore. At the rear is Frank Howse. (Photograph courtesy of Mrs. Sylvia Lavell)

In 1955 the commons was covered by a field of tents when Boy Scouts from around the world converged in Niagara for the World Jamboree.

In 1939, Brownies marched down King Street to see the King and Queen. Led by Miss Berge (Mrs. Gobert), from the right, are, Frances Thornton, Norma Alger, Ethel Gill, unidentified, Betty Clark, unidentified, Lillian Rundle, Eleanor Clark, unidentified, Sylvia Curtis, Aileen Cumpson, unidentified, Alma Jones, Amy Thornton, Betty Milne, Barbara Baker, and Marjorie Howarth. In the background, centre, is the Preservation Gallery on King Street.

Pictured here in 1922 are the Installation Officers of the Niagara District No. 22 Imperial Order of Odd Fellows. From left to right are the following: (front row) W.E. Stewart, W. Goldfinch, R. Slingerland, A. Sheppard, R. Vatcher, and T.W. McKeown; (back row) R. Lawson, P.D. Meadow, R.L. Prest, C. Woodruff, and N.K. McLeod. (Photograph courtesy of Sandra Woodruff)

The Janet Carnochan Chapter of the IODE (Imperial Order of the Daughters of the Empire) donated this ambulance to the Canadian Red Cross during the First World War. Miss Carnochan is seen here next to Sir Henry Pellat (far left).

During the Second World War, Newark Chapter IODE held weekly salvage drives to raise funds for the Navy League, for the Milk for British Children Fund, and for parcels for local servicemen and the crew of HMCS *Helena*. Pictured here at the salvage barn from left to right, are, Mesdames Librock, Bishop, Currie, D.S. Gordon, Smith, Hardison, Morgan, and P. Gordon.

These unidentified men are members and executives of the Niagara Branch Canadian Legion at the McDonald House on Queen Street in the 1930s. Branch 124 was founded in 1928. (Photograph courtesy of Mrs. Hester Kerr)

Veterans of the Fenian Raids are seen here in this Parade Float on July 1, 1927. From left to right, are, William Campbell, B.A. Taylor (Great War veteran and driver), John Thornton, and James Holohan.

This is the cast of a play put on by the Niagara Historical Society at St. Mark's Parish Hall.

83 QUEEN ST.

Theatre has long been a tradition in Niagara. The Kitchener building was constructed in 1916 as a vaudeville stage to entertain troops at Camp Niagara and many groups used the Court House for plays. The Shaw Festival now occupies both of these venues, plus the Festival Theatre. When George Reid purchased the venue *c*.1919, he renamed it the Royal George. The name changed again to the Brock Theatre (pictured here *c*.1940) around 1930. The Canadian Mime Company restored it in 1972 and reclaimed the name Royal George, which it retains to this day. (Photograph courtesy of Mrs. Patricia McCarthy)

Three
Getting to Niagara

This is the *Chicora,* one of the Niagara Navigation Company's steamships coming into Niagara past Fort Niagara. The ships travelled between Niagara and Toronto from 1877 until 1913 when several steamship companies formed Canada Steamship Lines. The ships of the Company were named; *Chicora, Cibola* (which burned in 1896), *Chippewa, Corona* (which replaced the *Cibola*) and *Cayuga.* The fleet would transport up to 10,000 visitors from Toronto to Niagara and Queenston on a busy summer weekend. Each of the four ships made two trips to Niagara daily in 1910.

The *Chicora* was built at Liverpool in 1864 to be used as a blockade runner for the Confederates during the American Civil War. She then spent several years on Lake Superior. She was bought by the Niagara Navigation Company in 1877 for service between their Toronto and Niagara ports. In this photograph the *Chicora* is in the foreground; the sails belong to other ships.

This later picture of the *Chicora* shows the ship as it was travelling between Toronto and Niagara. At this time the NNC had added a covered upper deck and new paddle-wheels. The *Chicora* operated this route from 1878 until just before the First World War.

Built by the Niagara Navigation Company in 1894, the *Chippewa* was one of the impressive steamers crossing the lake. It was 311 feet long with many luxuries on board including a salon that was 192 feet in length.

Shown here passing the dock area, headed upstream on its Niagara, Lewiston, Queenston, and Toronto run, the *Chippewa* retired in 1936 after forty-two years of service.

This wonderful photograph of the *Chippewa* is by local photographgrapher W.M. Quinn. Quinn, who produced many great images of Niagara, also made tintypes for tourists. Local stories tell us that the children of Niagara enjoyed sneaking up behind him and giving him a swift kick as he bent over the camera.

Wharf and harbor, Niagara-on-the-Lake, Canada.

The inner basin of the harbour area is well presented in this photograph. The Niagara-on-the-Lake Sailing Club now uses the harbour, but prior to that the basin was used by local commercial fishermen for launching their boats. The second Niagara lighthouse is in the middle of the photograph and you can make out Fort Niagara to the right.

The *Cayuga* was the most famous of the ships crossing Lake Ontario to Niagara. Built by Canadian Shipbuilding of Toronto, she was launched March 3, 1906. She was propelled by twin screws rather than paddles. The *Cayuga* serviced the lake until 1957. During her service, more than 15 million people travelled on the ship, the most famous being the Prince of Wales (later King Edward VIII) travelling from Toronto to Queenston in 1927.

This postcard shows the sentiment shared by many visitors who came to Niagara on the beautiful *Cayuga* steamship. The ship carried nearly 2,000 passengers and had a crew of seventy-five. Five round trip visits from Toronto to Niagara cost five dollars in 1913. Niagara residents also have sweet memories of the *Cayuga*, particularly of the ship's first trip of the season, usually May 24, when children travelled upriver for free.

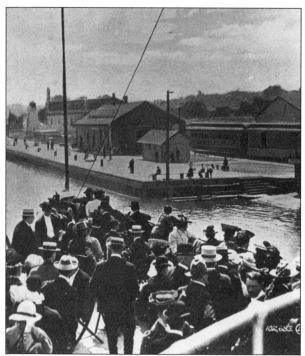

Arriving at Niagara, passengers would be entertained by young people diving off the high tower at the north end of the dock. There are other stories of children jumping into the wash of the *Cayuga* to dive for sinking coins thrown by passengers. In the upper photograph you can see the Michigan Central Train waiting for the ship to arrive at the wharf. Note the local children in swimsuits in the photograph below (bottom right corner).

Troops Disembarking for Niagara Camp

Ships plying between the Niagara Wharf and Toronto had no shortage of customers after Camp Niagara opened in 1872 as a training ground. Troops were frequently seen on the Wharf, coming from all points to stay in Niagara for a few days before heading back to their hometowns. During the First World War, for many soldiers, Camp Niagara was their last contact with their homes before heading to the war front.

Much more than just the passenger ships used the wharf area. Locals were very enterprising when it came to making money from the summer visitors. This is the steam tug *Abino* owned by Joseph Masters and his brothers. They used the boat to fish, but also taxied people between the dock area and Paradise Grove for ten cents per person. The Grove was a picnicking area on the Fort George Reserve that had a pavilion and swings for those who wanted to get away from it all.

Tourists filled the steamers coming to Niagara and local fruit filled the ship on its way back. Thousands of baskets of fruit were transported to the Toronto Wholesale Fruit Market in high season. Farmers loaded their baskets onto four-tiered wagons that were then wheeled across the gangplank to the lower deck.

This photograph was taken from the balcony of the American Hotel around 1935. It shows the hundreds of visitors who poured into town on every ship. The commercial fishing boats can also be seen in the basin. Ted and Goring Ball were the last commercial fishermen on Lake Ontario out of Niagara. They were third-generation fishermen in Niagara. Nets were set eight to ten miles offshore to catch either whitefish or blue pickerel. Lake trout, yellow pickerel, and sturgeon were also caught occasionally.

The nets of a commercial fisherman are seen here in 1906. (Photograph courtesy of Archives of Ontario)

The owner of the horse-drawn Erie and Ontario Railroad was Samuel Zimmerman. He purchased the Niagara Harbour and Dock Company in 1853 for £9,000 and set out to build an empire of steamships and trains that brought visitors to Niagara Falls and merchandise and fruit to Toronto and Buffalo. The Dock Company's foundry assisted with the construction of railway cars and Zimmerman worked with the town to get a loan of £25,000 to construct the railway. The line opened in 1854. This became a very successful endeavour for Zimmerman, but his untimely death in the Desjardins Canal (near Hamilton) railway accident in 1857 spelled the end of his company.

This 1894 photograph shows a group of visitors arriving to attend St. Andrew's Presbyterian Church Centennial.

This 1911 photograph of the Melville Street wharf shows the train station for the Michigan Central Railway (MCR) with a train departing. It was vital for the Niagara Navigation Company to have the connecting trains of the Michigan Central whisk visitors off to Niagara Falls and other destinations. This logical partnership didn't start off smoothly and took years to nurture because of contracts with other steamers.

The MCR Train is seen here on King Street with Field's Drug Store on the left *c*.1910. The rail line from Chippawa to Queenston was extended to Niagara in 1854. By 1910, five MCR trains ran daily to Buffalo during the summer months. (Photograph courtesy of *The Niagara Falls Review*)

This 1923 postcard shows the MCR train at its Queen Street station beside the Hotel Niagara. Train crews often stayed at the hotel, which is now the Prince of Wales Hotel. Train service was curtailed by 1923, probably because of competition from automobiles. (Photograph courtesy of John Burtniak)

Between 1913 and 1931 the electric streetcar connected the people of Niagara with St. Catharines. It provided the inhabitants of Niagara with many shopping opportunities in St. Catharines. Some high school students in Niagara took the streetcar to school in St. Catharines because Niagara did not offer a full choice of classes.

This picture shows the electric streetcar approaching its station at the corner of King and Market Streets. (Photograph courtesy of Mrs. Sandra M. Woodruff)

Railway transportation was not always the safest way to get around. In October 1913 the Michigan Central Railroad express, on its way to Niagara, hit an open switch near Queenston. The engine tender and two passenger cars left the track and the fireman was fatally injured. (Photograph courtesy of Mr. and Mrs. T.A. Clifford)

The Freel Brothers were conductors for the Niagara Central Railway. They are posing for this photograph on King Street. (Photograph courtesy of Mr. and Mrs. Henry Freel)

In the 1830s and 1840s industry in the dock area drove the booming economy of Niagara. In 1927 the wharf was still a commercial area. This photograph shows the Riverside Hotel, the coal chute used to refuel the steamers, the railway station, and the Canada Steamship Lines freight shed in the distance.

This photograph shows the inner harbour boat-building slip at Niagara. The building fronting Melville Street is the American Hotel. The small building opposite the American was used to store small boats and wood. The tall building behind is the 1921 basket factory of T.B. Rivett and the United Growers Co-operative, which became the Keenan Woodenware building in 1925. Though no longer used as a factory, wooden baskets were stored in the building. When it burned in 1961, they created a spectacular blaze.

The 1891 Pumphouse on Ricardo Street, shown on the right of this *c.*1904 photograph, is a fine example of industrial architecture. Built during the late nineteenth and early twentieth century boom period, its pumps supplied the town with water from the Niagara River until 1983. The steam pumps also generated electricity for the growing town. The lighthouse is seen on the left side of the photograph. Both buildings still stand today.

Built in 1904 by Marine and Fisheries Canada, the fog alarm building, located on River Beach road, was used in foggy weather to guide ships to port. One of the very few original foghorn houses still standing in the province, it remains a symbol of Niagara's days as a busy lake port.

Ice Jam at Niagara Apr 26th 1909

The Ice Jam of April 1909 occurred when seven miles of ice came over the Falls and down the Niagara River. Towers of ice up to forty feet high were recorded; wharfs (like McIntyre's Wharf shown here in these two pictures) were pushed off their piles and newspapers reported hundreds of thousands of dollars worth of damage to property along the riverbank.

ICE JAM APRIL 29 09, SHOWING LIGHT HOUSE AND NIAGARA WHARF.

For more than twenty days, the ice threatened the Niagara Wharf. It finally broke completely free on April 29, 1909. In the end, every wharf and dock along the lower river was completely destroyed except for the Niagara dock. There would have been a considerable loss to the tourism economy of Niagara-on-the-Lake, the Niagara Navigation Company, and Michigan Central Railway had the wharf given way to the enormous stress placed upon it.

Four
Heritage Houses and Grand Estates

The superb 1820s residential block between Gate and Simcoe Streets, seen here in 1890, remains largely intact in 2003, except for the removal of the three-story building right of center, which was an 1833 addition to the early block. From right to left, the four houses shown are the Rogers-Harrison, the Crysler-McDougal, the Peabody-Anderson, and the Crysler-Rigg. Note the hitching posts and the plank crossings from the unpaved street to the entrance of the buildings. In 2005 the rear wing of the Peabody-Anderson House was torn down.

2UEEN ST.

Built soon after the War of 1812 by the Rogers, a family of innkeepers and merchants, this house was owned by the Rogers and their descendants, the Blakes and the Harrisons until the 1990s. The six-bay clapboard house covered in stucco, lined to resemble cut stone, retains much of its original exterior detail. This photograph is dated 1890.

157 QUEEN ST.

165 QUEEN ST.

In 1820, merchant Adam Crysler built this fine brick townhouse with double arcades and elaborate door case. His heirs sold the property in 1849 to Colonel Daniel McDougal, a veteran of the Battle of Lundy's Lane, treasurer of Lincoln, Welland and Haldimand counties, and a founding member of the St. Vincent de Paul congregation. The Harrison family, who lived next door, acquired the house in the 1920s and it is still owned by their descendants.

Mary Agnes Blake was the daughter of John Blake and Mary Ann Rogers. John Blake died in 1835 and so Mary Agnes and her younger brother were raised in the Rogers' house by their mother and uncles. The children were musical and often performed in concerts for charity. This 1850 photograph shows Agnes at the age of eighteen. She later married Duncan McFarland.

Willie McDougal Newton was the brilliant, but eccentric grandson of Colonel Daniel McDougal. He founded the *Echo of Niagara* (1884), a short-lived and controversial newspaper noted for its barbed editorials, and also wrote for the *Niagara Falls Review* and for U.S. papers. He lived in the McDougal home with his mother from 1883 until her death in 1915 when he became a recluse, occupying a small cottage behind the house. This photograph is from the 1860s.

The nucleus of this house was built as a store for watchmaker Tenny Peabody in 1820. However, its best-known occupants were banker Thomas McCormick and physician Hedley Anderson, owner at the time of this 1900 photograph. From 1920 to 1951 the building was the town's Cottage Hospital; many residents of Niagara were born here. The asphalt siding (which now covers the original cladding) and a rear wing were added during this period.

175 QUEEN ST.

Merchant Ralph M. Crysler built a two-story, neoclassical frame building in 1822, to which lawyer Charles L. Hall added the southeast wing and balcony in 1840. In the twentieth century, several American summer residents owned the house. They included George K. Birge of Buffalo (1895-1903) who added more galleries, Page M. Baker (1903-1910), publisher of the *New Orleans Times* who named the house Roslyn Cottage, and Cleveland railway magnate Donald R. MacBain and family (1919-1952). The photograph is from 1900.

187 QUEEN ST.

Dr. Hedley Leeming Anderson, a native of Fort Erie, practiced in Niagara from 1875 until his retirement in 1919, often as the town's sole physician. Revered by his patients and the press, he was known as "Niagara's beloved physician" and "the people's best friend." He owned 175 Queen Street from 1889-1919. He is pictured here with his family.

Lawyer Charles L. Hall (1817-1849) came to Niagara from Sandwich (Windsor) to practice at the Court House. An active speculator in property, he kept an annotated plan of the town, showing names of lot owners. He married Miss Amelia Downes, a sister of Mrs. Robert Melville. His descendants lived in the Crysler house until 1888.

Shown in 1890 is the front entrance of the Richardson house, built in 1822 for Charles Richardson, a young barrister, M.L.A., brother of Canadian novelist John Richardson and nephew of the first Mrs. Robert Hamilton. Occupying an acre of land at the corner of Queen and Simcoe Streets, it is the only dwelling on the Mississauga Reserve.

209 QUEEN ST.

The early Richardson building was enlarged in the town's late nineteenth-century summer resort period, by Garrie Humphrey Birge of Buffalo who hired Niagara builder John Ellison to add the galleries, then in vogue with American owners. The property has had several names. A.K. Silverthorne, owner in 1900 when this photograph was taken, called it Green Acres; the Gooderham family renamed it Nenagh Hall; and from 1920-87 it was known as the Kiely house. The Kiely name was retained after its sale and conversion to a Heritage Inn in 1987.

A plaque on the boulevard of 130 Front Street commemorates Canadian author William Kirby who, in 1857, bought this house, built in 1832. It was he who added the porch and French windows seen in this 1895 photograph. His descendants lived here until after World War One. He described the town as "as near Heaven as any town whatever."

British-born William Kirby (1817-1906) was quite active in the Niagara community. The third editor of the *Niagara Mail* (published 1846-70) and later Collector of Customs, he was also a member of the School Board, president of the library for twenty-five years, Honorary President of the Niagara Historical Society, and a strong supporter of the work of Maria Rye (see Chapter two "Our Western Home").

This white clapboard building, known as the Captain's House, was built in 1818 by carpenter John Brauer for Major Thomas Evans, officer at Fort George in 1817-19 (later promoted to Major General and awarded a K.C.B). However, the house was named for Captain Edward Oates, Master of the Richmond Packet who leased it so that his wife could watch for his ship returning across the lake. In 1866 and 1867, John C. Breckinridge occupied the house. One of a group of Confederate refugees in Niagara after the U.S. Civil War, he too, appreciated the view from the verandah, though *his* focus was the American fort. Much later, a family named Richmond occupied the dwelling and called it the Richmond House, a name with links to both Oates and its Confederate occupants.

80 FRONT ST.

The nucleus of 10 Front Street. was built in 1817 for Thomas Racey, a town warden. Samuel Street, an influential entrepreneur owned it from 1825-54 and Lewis Shickluna, a noted boat builder, from 1854-73. It is said that a barn on the property had "Savings Bank" stencilled in gilt letters on its King Street façade. Traces of a vault were still evident in the basement in 1990 – hence its popular name, "The Old Bank House." The verandah is a late Victorian addition. Several other additions are post 1990.

This fine house on King Street. opposite Simcoe Park was built in 1880 by Walter Davidson for Samuel Rowley, a glass manufacturer from Philadelphia, and his wife Fanny. Fanny was the granddaughter of William Riley, a slave who escaped from Virginia in 1802 and joined the black community in town. He lived in a small log cabin on Mary Street. Fanny's house is now the Preservation Gallery.

177 KING ST.

The Dover house, a small board and batten salt box, is situated on Platoff Street on New Survey land southeast of King Street, which was added to the town in 1823. It was built on a lot owned in 1838 by Thomas Dover, for whom it is named. In this 1900 photograph, Jenny Patterson poses on the plank path. The house was restored *c.*1970 and rooms were added in 2003.

John Carnochan, brother of Janet, built this house in 1884 on New Survey land at the corner of Wellington and Platoff. Seven years later, he sold the property to Janet, who occupied the dwelling for some years.

Fifty-eight Johnson Street. was built in 1830 by contractor Ed McMullen, and refurbished in the 1870s by ship's carpenter Robert Fizette. However, the house is known as the Eckersley house for John Eckersley a retired civil servant from Nova Scotia who bought the property in 1902. Eckersley is seen here with his second wife Georgina. The porch shown in the photograph encroached on town property. Its removal in 1907 following a bitter battle waged by Eckersley against town council left a "suicide door" over the front entrance until 1964 when his daughters sold the property.

Shoemaker George Flynn built this house c.1860 on Johnson Street, on land given to him by his mother, who operated a recess (off license) next door on King Street. Its best-known early owners were the Flanigans, whose two daughters Bella and Minnie were noted for their fashionable dress. In 1881 extensive alterations were made to the house, probably by John Carnochan who married Bella. In the Second World War the Knights of Columbus used the building to entertain troops from the army camp.

Situated on a four-acre natural oasis, owned by the Claus family from 1799-1859, 407 King Street was built in 1816-17 by William Claus, Deputy Superintendent of the Indian Department. It is said to have been modelled on Napoleon's "house of exile" in St. Helena. Claus left diaries recording not only the progress of the building, but also the planting of flowers, trees, and vines in the extensive grounds. In 1919 the property, known as the Wilderness, was bought by W.R. Austin, whose daughter Mrs. Parker became owner in 1925. She and her daughters, who still own the Wilderness, have faithfully preserved the historically significant estate.

In 1817 William Duff Miller, who owned a stationery store on Queen Street and also served for over thirty years as Deputy Clerk at the second Court House (later Miss Rye's school), built this house on Mary Street, conveniently located between his two places of business. The Miller family owned the house until 1870 before selling it to Mr. and Mrs. William Hewgill, who retained it until the turn of the century when this photograph was taken.

46 MARY ST.

William Duff Miller (1786 – 1859) devoted many of his non-working hours to the Presbyterian Church where he was session clerk for forty-two years and elder for twenty-nine. He was credited with keeping the congregation united in the years from 1805 to 1829 when St. Andrew's lacked a permanent minister.

In 1817, John Breakenridge, a Virginia lawyer noted for his good taste, built 392 Mississauga Street, a large frame house situated on a 1 1/8-acre estate lot. The 1902 photograph shows the house from the side, revealing the kitchen wing added in 1840 and the new porch and balcony added by Captain C.S. Herring, owner from 1900-1950. Partly visible behind the front pillars is Breakenridge's fine doorcase—the feature that first attracted Frank Hawley, who bought the house (in urgent need of repair) in 1953. Mr. Hawley, a member of the first board of the Ontario Heritage Foundation, meticulously restored the entire house to its early eighteenth century elegance.

The large Tudor Revival house at the corner of Simcoe and Queen Streets was built in 1914 by contractor W. Edwin Lee and designed by Charles Wilmot, the architect of the 1922 War Memorial Clock Tower. The owner of the house was Joseph M. Mussen, former Canadian trade commissioner in England, prime promoter of the Clock Tower, and Lord Mayor of the town. In this 1915 photograph are, at the left, Mr. and Mrs. Watts Lansing and second from the right, Joseph Mussen. Mr. and Mrs. John Drope owned the house from 1965-86.

Agnes McGaw (later Mrs Goodwin N. Bernard), daughter of an owner of the Queen's Royal and sister of Mrs. Mussen, built the house shortly before the First World War, next door to the Mussens on Queen Street. Captain Bert James Dayton bought it in 1943 and named it The Gables. Dentist Leslie Bannister was the owner from 1946-86 when he sold it to Mr. and Mrs. R. Mori. (Photograph Courtesy of Miss Valentine Onslow Collection)

The house at 284 Queen Street is an outstanding example of the elegant summer estates owned by wealthy Americans in the late nineteenth and early twentieth centuries. The large clapboard dwelling with spacious verandahs was built in 1899 by Watts Sherman Lansing of Buffalo and Niagara, one of several houses he built in town between 1887 and 1906. In 1906 he sold the house with two acres of landscaped gardens and orchards and a barn large enough for two horses to Charles Weston, a multi-millionaire lumber baron. The Weston heirs owned the estate until 1963 when they sold it to Leicester C. Forster.

In 1895 Gustav Fleischman, a wealthy Buffalo distiller, bought a four-acre block facing the lake and golf course, with an existing house built in 1890 near the corner of Dorchester Street. The following year he employed John Ellison to add an east wing, a large front verandah, and upper balconies. An 1896 newspaper praised the refurbished summer house – seen in this *c.*1900 photograph – as "the most complete in position, comfort and appointment of the whole." Mr. Fleischman named his estate Clarette, a tribute to his two oldest daughters, Clara and Henrietta. In 1908 Henrietta's wedding reception, held at the house, was described in detail in *The Times* of June 19th. Conrad Wettlauffer, a Buffalo physician, bought Clarette in 1912. Two years later he altered the house, reducing the number of rooms and enlarging them to accommodate their frequent house parties. Mr. Wettlauffer also divided the lot, adding a second house near the corner of Butler Street for his son, Taylor. In 1966, his heirs sold the house, stripped of its early towers and galleries, to Mr. and Mrs. Harris. Renamed Lakewinds, it was bought in 1994 by Mr. and Mrs. S. Locke, who refurbished the house and transformed the grounds into one of the town's finest gardens.

In 1798 William Dickson, merchant, lawyer and M.L.A., bought 160 acres fronting on present-day John Street from Lieutenant Governor Simcoe's successor as administrator of Upper Canada, Hon. Peter Russell. On part of this land are Randwood and its neighbour Brunswick Place, two estates which are representative of both Niagara's second blossoming as a late nineteenth-century resort town, and of its rebirth from the ashes of the burning in 1813. Dickson gave ten acres to his oldest son Robert, who in 1823 built a three-bay, two-story brick house with centre hall on the estate. (Painting by Hopner Meyer)

In 1873, retired U.S. General Henry Lansing, Niagara's pioneer summer resident, bought the Dickson house and added the mansard roof, the closed tower, and the verandah with twin slender posts shown in this 1895 photograph. Both Dickson and Lansing called the estate Woodlawn.

In 1905, George F. Rand, a self-made millionaire and philanthropist, bought Woodlawn and renamed it Randwood. The Rand family added an east-side solarium, opened the tower, recreated the verandah, and built the enclosing stone wall, fountain, and pool in front of the house. These changes are apparent in this c.1940 photograph.

176 JOHN ST.

H.P.BISSELL.

The site of Brunswick Place was William Dickson's gift to his second son, William. William Junior sold these 10 acres of land to Robert Melville, an officer at Fort George who became the first manager of the Niagara Harbour and Dock Company. In 1830, Melville built the three-bay house with elaborate doorcase, shown in this 1900 photograph, and called it Brunswick Place. Other pre-1900 owners included Robert George Dickson, Hon. William's grandson, who renamed the estate Pinehurst (because it contained 200 pine trees planted by Melville), and Buffalo barrister Herbert Bissell. Twentieth-century owners Charles and Harriet Greiner (1902-22) and Edward H. and Ruth Abbott Letchworth (1928-65) refurbished and extended Melville's home. From the 1930s through the 1950s, the Rands and the Letchworths made their part of John Street a centre of the summer scene in Niagara.

210 JOHN ST

Five
Leisurely Pursuits

Local boys in Niagara often found jobs at the Niagara Golf Club caddying for the wealthy visitors to town. This playful group had their photograph taken in 1902. "Rules for Caddies at the Niagara Golf Club. There will be two classes of caddies. First class must have good sight and a good understanding of the Links and games and be well behaved. They will earn $0.25/round. Second class is all others who wish to carry clubs and will earn $0.20/round. All caddies must deposit $1 at the beginning of the year to guarantee good behaviour."

From its inception, golf has been a popular sport in Niagara. Charles Hunter (left) is pictured on the Fort George Golf Course in 1887. Mr. Hunter and J. Geale Dickson laid out the first golf course in Niagara, the Fort George Course, in 1877. The next year they made a course on the Fort Mississauga Common. Mr. Hunter was a fixture at the course for years and greatly influenced the expansion of the sport in Niagara. The course on the Fort Mississauga Common is the oldest course still in use in North America.

The Fort George Course Club House was in the Officer's Quarters, which was built in 1820. It can be seen here at the close of the International Golf Tournament of 1902.

NIAGARA RIVER NEAR FORT GEORGE
NIAGARA ON THE LAKE

These two photographs show different holes of the Fort George Course. The bottom is "The Willows" or sixteenth hole. One newspaper, when describing a round on this course in the late 1890s, stated "a pony cart followed them from hole to hole laden with every possible beverage which the human tongue could desire."

Miss Madeleine Geale was an extraordinary local golfer. She was very instrumental in the early years of the golf course, holding down the position of Secretary of the Niagara Golf Club. It was most unusual for a woman to hold such a title at the time. This is most likely attributable to her success on the course and in the local tournaments. One newspaper article discussed her ability and her celebrity among golfers noting that, "The Niagara lady made her fame as possessing the prettiest golf stroke among women in America." Miss Geale backed this up on the course. She competed in the first ever Niagara International Tournament in 1895 and won the ladies division. She posted a score of 65 for nine holes. Her opponent was Mrs. Hobart Chatfield-Taylor of Chicago who scored a 71.

Niagara has been home to several winning hockey teams, including this one. Pictured from left to right, (front row) John Campbell, Dick Reid, John Hartley; (middle row) Frank Walsh, Fred McClelland, Bob Patterson; (back row) Joe Dorrity, Bill Curtis, Charlie Bishop, and Charlie Sherlock. Local folklore abounds with stories of firsts in hockey history. It is possible that Dick Reid may have been one of the first people to splice a piece of wood onto his stick and create a longer one. Previously, sticks were roughly the same size as modern day field hockey sticks.

This photograph was taken just before the First World War. The players whose names we know include Hedley Reid, Felix Lynch, George MacCarter, Art Masters and Ed Richardson.

The NOTL Lawn Bowling Club was organised in 1877 and played at the Queen's Royal until 1922 when it moved to a new facility at the corners of Regent and Johnson.

This photograph shows the lawn bowling activities at the Queen's Royal. The corner of King and Front Streets can be seen in the top right of the picture.

This view of the ladies Lawn Bowling Club is from the corner of Front and King Streets. The Queen's Royal Hotel is just beyond the cluster of trees on the far side of the green. The building in the picture was the Hotel Annex.

The lawn tennis court was the same field that was used for lawn bowling at the Queen's Royal Hotel. The Hotel organised every type of event imaginable to attract visitors. The International Golf, Bowling, and Tennis Tournaments were the most significant. Players from near and far competed on the grounds overlooking the Niagara River, Lake Ontario, and Fort Niagara. This photograph was taken during the International Tennis Tournament of 1898.

During the late nineteenth and early twentieth century, Niagara-on-the-Lake held the Niagara International Tennis Tournament, the oldest tennis event in Canada. The last week of August was dedicated to the grand spectacle of the greatest Canadian and American players coming to town to compete. Admission to the event in 1896 was twenty-five cents and a badge for the entire tournament cost one dollar. Tournament balls, dances, boating parties, and other activities made "the evening hours slip by on golden wings of pleasure." The bottom photograph is of a championship match (*c.*1910) between Miss May Sutton (foreground) and Mrs. Hannam (Canadian Champion) of Toronto. Miss Sutton won the match. (Top photograph courtesy of Francis Petrie Collection)

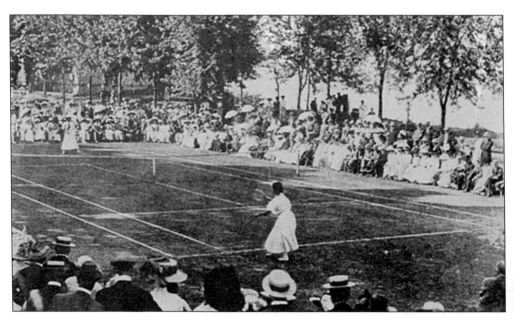

Cyclists from all parts of America came to Niagara to compete in the Bicycle Gymkhana. The first day usually featured a grand parade at the Queen's Royal Hotel with decorated bicycles, followed by boys and girls racing. On the second day the real competitions began. There were many interesting races during the tournament. The Maiden's Scurry was for girls under age sixteen who needed to start, turn, go over an obstacle eighteen inches high—over which the wheel must be lifted—and finish. To win the Obstacle Race, one was required to start, ride ten yards, dismount, lift the wheel over an obstacle, ride thirty yards, pick up a handkerchief without dismounting, ride twenty yards, go over a hurdle and finish. There was also the Tortoise Race where the winner was the last person to cover the fifty-yard course without falling off his or her bicycle. This photograph portrays some Gymkhana prize winners c.1900.

The views of Ryerson Park (above) and the Niagara River (below) show how popular boating on Lake Ontario was to locals and tourists. Fishing was a very popular activity for tourists. A souvenir map from 1894 shows that one of the best fishing holes was straight across the river near the banks of Fort Niagara.

At one time, Niagara had six boat liveries: one between the two steamboat wharves, one below Rousseau's Wharf, two at the foot of King Street, one at the beach, and one on the grounds of the Queen's Royal Hotel.

John Redhead had boat liveries at Rousseau's Wharf and at the Foot of King Street. Redhead built his own boats, which were trimmed with black walnut or cherry wood. He had up to forty-five boats in use at once. This is a photograph of one of his liveries.

Visitors to Niagara mostly came from the expanding cities of Canada and the United States. The cool waters of Lake Ontario were a very nice treat compared to the heat of the cities in the summer.

This postcard shows several swimmers at the beach at the foot of King Street with Fort Niagara in the background.

Oak Grove was renamed Paradise Grove by the MCR when they started running a spur line to this cluster of trees just beyond the Fort George Military Reserve. Visitors often had picnics at the Grove under the massive black oak and occasional large white oak trees. This photograph is from October 1889.

This unknown group of people is posing for a photograph in Ryerson Park, which is in the Chautauqua area of town. It was near Lake Ontario and One Mile Creek (referred to as Landsdowne Lake at the time) where people could picnic, go for a row in the creek, swim, or fish.

Park areas were available for picnics and fun around town. This postcard shows the popular swings that were in Simcoe Park at the turn of the century.

Folklore states that Bois le Grand brought from France a branch of the holy thorn, brought by Pope Clement from Palestine, which supplied the Saviour's crown of thorns. The French occupied Fort Niagara from 1725 until 1759 and frequently came to the west side of the Niagara River. It was on one of these trips that Le Grand planted these thorns on the area that is now known as the Commons near Fort George. The legend goes even further and states that all thorn trees in the area derive from these two trees.

Six

Military

The first <u>Navy Hall</u> was actually a complex of storage buildings, barracks, and workshops for the Provincial Marine. There were four or five buildings and they served this function from *c.*1765 to the 1780s. One building was fitted up in 1792 as Executive Council chambers, offices, and the residence for Lieutenant Governor John Graves Simcoe. This photograph was taken in 1909, before the building was restored three years later. In 1914, typhoid was a problem in town. Navy Hall was used as a lab to test water used at Camp Niagara. It was also an inoculation clinic during the First World War.

The Powder Magazine is the only fort building that survived the bombardment of Fort George on May 25, 1813. It was built between 1796-1799. The original magazine had buttresses, which were dismantled and rebuilt in 1893. The walls are 4 feet thick.

Old Fort Mississauga, Built 1814, Niagara-on-the-Lake, Canada.

When the British reoccupied Niagara in December 1813, the town was in ruins following the fires set on December 10 by the retreating U.S. forces. In the spring of 1814, the British began strengthening the battery position of Mississauga point by constructing Fort Mississauga, an irregular star-shaped fort that featured a stone Martello-type tower. The tower and magazines built into the earthworks incorporated stone and brick rubble salvaged from the town and from the nearby lighthouse. The fort was occupied until 1865 during times of international and national threats. The bottom photograph shows golfers on the nine-hole golf course constructed on the military reserve area surrounding Fort Mississauga. (Bottom photograph courtesy of Archives of Ontario)

This photograph from 1865 shows the Queen's Own Regiment forming a Square on the Commons near Butlers Barracks. The Queen's Own formed a square at the Battle of Ridgeway in 1866 and were vulnerable to long-range Fenian rifle fire, which forced the regiment to quickly retreat from the field. In the background of this photograph is the Military Hospital that was built in 1822.

These 1865 photographs shows the Niagara Company Volunteers in the Niagara market square, which is located behind the buildings on the south side of Queen Street. Note the Angel Inn in the centre of the upper photograph. The lower photograph shows 1860s structures on Regent Street, the building on the right of this photograph still stands today. (Photographs courtesy of Mrs. Sandra M. Woodruff)

Number One Company of Niagara Volunteers in 1866. The photograph faintly shows St. Vincent de Paul Church on the left and Doyle's Hotel on the right.

These are some Niagara volunteers on active service in Fort Erie during the Fenian Raids of 1866. Identified in the photograph are Captain E. Thompson, Lieutenant R. Currie, Ensign Johnson Clench, George Ellison, and James Matthews. This may be a photograph of an officers' mess in the field or a whiskey seller's booth.

These two photographs, taken in 1872, overlook Camp Niagara on the commons, or Military Reserve. The Camp operated until 1967 with limited use after the Second World War. The top photograph shows the Public School on the left of the photograph. The bottom photograph shows the Public School (right) and a racecourse in the middle of the field. It was on this course that some of the officers raced their horses.

British troops were withdrawn from Canada in 1870-71 after provisions were made to train the militia of Upper Canada. In June 1871 the commons was converted to a large-scale summer militia training camp called Camp Niagara. Camp Niagara brought a steady stream of troops to Niagara. Militia corps from all over Ontario arrived by steamer or by train almost every summer for ninety years.

The duality of summer visitors to Niagara is best explored in this photograph. The Junior Commissariat Officer's Quarters near Butler's Barracks (no longer occupied) was converted into the Fort George Golf Course Clubhouse. The soldiers were definitely grateful that the government chose a training facility that was next to a town with lots of activities. Businesses were booming because of the many visitors to town, both vacationers and soldiers.

The 44th Lincoln and Welland Regiment at Camp Niagara, posing for a group photograph on June 16, 1899. From left to right are as follows: (sitting) Captain F. W. Hill, Major Clark, Lieutenant Harcourt, Major J.E. Cohe, and Lieutenant McCallum; (kneeling) Lieutenant D.J.C. Munro, Captain Evely (#4 Coy), T. Ch. Mitchell, and Major H. Bender; (standing) Lieutenant Cowper (Surgeon), Lieutenant W.W. Thompson, Lt. Allan (QOR), Captain H.A. Rose, #5 Lieutenant Colonel E.A. Cruikshank, Captain Gibson, Reverend Dr. Johnstone (Honorary Chaplain), Lieutenant Cline, Lieutenant Laur, Captain Vandersluys, and Captain Greenwood.

At Camp Niagara, June 3, 1903 the 44th Lincoln and Welland Regiment Officers from left to right, are, (sitting) unidentified,Captain Evely #4 Coy,Captain James E. Laur, Major J.A. Vandersluys, VD, Lieutenant Colonel E.A. Cruikshank, Major John Eda Cohoe, Captain Surgeon W.W. Thompson, Capt. Adjutant Fred W. Hill, Major Charles Herring, and unidentified; (standing) Captain H. R. Rose, unidentified, Captain Gibson, W.F., Major D.J.C. Munro, five unidentified men, Captain Greenwood, and #3 Coy John A.

This photograph shows the Artillery Camp in 1908. Militia training was generally twelve days of drilling and manoeuvres. The soldiers definitely improved the local economy during these training sessions in Niagara.

After the Boer War, there was a move to abandon Camp Niagara because of limited size. In 1908 the Federal government purchased more land along the lakeshore and moved the rifle range outside of the town. This photograph shows the vehicles (horses in the background and wagons in the forefront) that the troops used to move around supplies between the Boer War and the First World War.

The presence of troops in Niagara was very apparent during the First World War. The top photograph shows an Army Band marching down Queen Street. In June 1914 there were 2,500 soldiers at Camp Niagara. The local paper reported that the police chief was "shooing away tramps and camp followers." The bottom picture is from 1915. (Bottom photograph courtesy of *The Niagara Falls Review*)

Camp Niagara Headquarters Staff, of the First World War, from left to right, are, (sitting on the ground) Captain Bruce, Captain Benoit; (sitting) Lieutenant Colonel Thairs, Lieutenant Colonel Pellatt, Lieutenant Colonel Denison, General Otter, Lieutenant Colonel Galloway, Lieutenant Colonel Hall, and Lieutenant Colonel Fotheringham; (standing) Captain Telford, Major Van Nostran, Major Langton, Lieutenant Colonel Harston, Major Macdonald, Captain Shanly, and Captain Harbottle.

Bugle Band of 44th Lincoln and Welland Regiment, was the largest at Camp Niagara during the First World War. The 44th was combined with the 19th Lincoln Regiment in 1936 to form the Lincoln and Welland Regiment, which is our current local regiment.

This is the 37th Regiment Band at Camp Niagara. The 37th was known as the Haldimand Rifles and was entirely Native Canadian.

77th (Wentworth) Regiment with Butler's Barracks in the Background. This photograph was taken during the First World War.

Butler's Barracks were named after Colonel John Butler who is one of the founders of Niagara and Ontario. Butler built two ranges of barracks, one where Chateau Gardens now stands, the other near this site. These buildings were destroyed prior to the War of 1812. Following the war, this area became the main barrack and depot for Niagara, replacing Fort George. The name Butler's Barracks was retained for the entire complex. This 1927 photograph shows the 1815 Soldiers Barracks, which today houses the Lincoln and Welland Regimental Museum.

This car belonged to Major W.E.S. Knowles. In the car with him are Lieutenant Colonel Ptolemy, Major Orr, and Captain Hagar, all officers of the 77th Regiment. The car was very handy during First World War training. Its headlights were used to light the area for the distribution of rations at the bivouac on Queenston Heights during the "sham fight."

This view of the Canadian Expeditionary Force encampment out on the Military Reserve is taken from the top of the Fort Mississauga tower looking towards town. Camp Niagara was so active during the First World War that tents covered the Commons, the Fort Mississauga commons, and the grounds of Fort George, forcing closure of the golf courses on the two commons. This caused enormous headaches for Henry Winnett; with the Forces camped on the golf courses, guests at his Queen's Royal Hotel lacked activities. Winnett, in a letter to the Mayor of Niagara claimed that, "My opinion of Niagara-on-the-Lake is that it never can be anything but a summer resort and without good golf it won't amount to a 'hill of beans'."

The Aldershot Ovens at Camp Niagara are from the First World War. Large fires were built in the semi-circular steel ovens. Once the wood had burned down, the coals and ashes were withdrawn and the roasting pans or bread pans put in.

Beginning in September 1917, camps were organized on the Niagara commons to provide two months of training for Polish volunteers recruited in the United States. The objective was to prepare them for a Polish army, which was quietly being assembled in France in order to free Poland from foreign rule. In November 1917 there were over 4,000 volunteers in camp. The camps were multinational efforts. The French government paid volunteers five cents a day and promised an annual bonus of $150. The American Red Cross and the YMCA provided recreation tents and the Buffalo Polish-American Citizens Organization helped clothe, feed, and transport the men to Niagara. Canadian officers supervised the training and many town residents provided free accommodation during the winter of 1917. By the time the last camp closed in March 1919, over 22,000 men had been trained and 21,000 of them had been sent to France to serve in the Polish Blue Army—so named because of their distinctive light-blue uniforms. In July 1918, the world-renowned pianist, Jan Paderewski, who later became the Premier of free Poland, and his wife Helena visited the Niagara camp. He is seen here inspecting the troops.

In 1918, the Polish trainees held an enthusiastic Armistice Day celebration, marching across the commons and through the town. Janet Carnochan described the parade as "the most wonderful sight" with cannons, "cages for the Kaiser, and unique disguises," and colourful flags, including the Polish White Eagle (the old flag of free Poland).

When deadly influenza swept through the camp in the winter of 1918-19, forty-one Polish soldiers fell victim to the epidemic. Over twenty of them are buried in the cemetery of St. Vincent de Paul in a special plot donated by the church and enclosed by an ornamental wrought-iron fence. In June 1919 Polish residents of Buffalo came to Niagara in a special railway car to hold a memorial service and decorate each grave. From this event sprang the tradition of the annual Polish pilgrimage to Niagara-on-the-Lake on the first Sunday of June.

These two postcards are from 1942. The Camp appears to be quite large, but at the end of the Second World War, the camp was deemed to be too small and some of the buildings were sold and towed away, while others were demolished. The camp did start up militia training again in 1953 but this was short lived, with the last training exercise held here in 1965.